Blending Coffee

Your Guide to Coffee Blends and the Perfect Cup

By

Jessica Simms

JESSICA SIMMS

Blending Coffee: Your Guide to Coffee Blends and the Perfect Cup

Copyright © 2017

All rights reserved. This book or any portion thereof may not be reproduced or used in any manner whatsoever without the express written permission of the publisher except for the use of brief quotations in a book review.

ISBN: 9781520895734

Warning and Disclaimer

Every effort has been made to make this book as accurate as possible. However, no warranty or fitness is implied. The information provided is on an "as-is" basis. The author and the publisher shall have no liability or responsibility to any person or entity with respect to any loss or damages that arise from the information in this book.

Publisher contact

Skinny Bottle Publishing

books@skinnybottle.com

SKINNY BOTTLE

More Than a Bean!... 1

Understanding Coffee Flavors 3

    Planting and growth 4

    Harvesting and processing... 7

    Roasting.. 9

The Flavor Wheel 11

    Using the wheel 13

Regional Profiles 19

    The Americas 20

    Africa 22

    Southeast Asia and Oceania... 23

The Artful Blend... 25

    Mocha Java 27

    Italian Blend 28

    Drip Brew Melange.. 29

    Espresso Melange 29

Flavored Coffees... 31

Extracts 33

Whole spices 33

Ground spices 34

Nuts 34

Fruit 35

Go Blend! 36

More Than a Bean!

To say that coffee is a bean is a bit of a misnomer. If you were to see a ripe coffee plant, you would find it covered in red berries; the part of the plant that is roasted, ground, and brewed into the beverage is the seed inside this fruit. Coffee trees can grow in a wide range of climates and elevations but they're predominantly grown in three regions of the world: Central and South America, Africa, and southeast Asia.

If all the beans in a bag of coffee come from the same growing region, it's known as a single-origin coffee. You'll typically see these labeled with a geographic name, like Guatemala Antigua or Ethiopia Yirgacheffe. They could also be named for their cultivar, especially if it's a particularly coveted one (e.g. Panama Geisha), or for the farm where they were grown. Because the flavor of coffee is greatly influenced by environmental factors like soil composition, elevation, and climate conditions, knowing where the beans were grown is often a good indication of its flavor notes and overall quality.

If the coffees in the bag come from a lot of different places, it's known as a blend. Some people have the misconception that blends are inherently lower in quality than single-origin coffees. Blends can be used to hide the flavor of inferior beans, but more often they're a way to add complexity to the final cup by pairing complementary flavors. Making your own blends at home can be a great way to customize your daily cup without investing in costly new equipment like a home roaster or espresso machine. While you'll get the most flavor from buying whole beans and grinding them yourself at home, you can also blend pre-ground coffee if you lack the necessary equipment (and the budget to obtain it).

In the not too distant past, the coffee section of most grocery stores was stocked almost exclusively by blends, most of them pre-ground. While this is changing, your best bet for finding a wide variety of single-origin coffees is still likely to be a café or roaster. The staff in these establishments works with coffee day in and day out, and they can answer any questions you have about their beans or point out roasts that seem suited to your tastes. When buying at the supermarket (or from the internet), your knowledge is often limited to what's printed on the package.

The main thing you need if you want to make your own blends is knowledge about coffee—how it develops its distinctive flavors, how to identify flavor notes, and how to figure out which beans will complement each other. The chapters that follow in this book will get you up to speed on everything you need to know to start making your own coffee blends at home.

Understanding Coffee Flavors

There are a lot of different factors that can influence the taste of the coffee in your cup, one of the main reasons it can seem so complicated to someone just getting into the intricacies of the beverage. Every stage of the process from planting to roasting leaves its mark on the flavor of the final brew. Depending on how it's grown, processed, and roasted, coffee can have a bright, citrusy flavor or a darker chocolatey or nutty taste; its texture can be sharp like tea or lingering and syrupy. The fact that so much variation is possible is what makes coffee blending such a complex and fascinating art.

Understanding just what gives certain coffees their distinctive flavor profiles is the first step toward mastering the art of blending. It lets you make informed decisions about which beans and roast levels will complement each other. There are three basic stages to a coffee bean's development: the growth, the processing, and the roasting. Each of these stages is explored in more depth in the sections that follow.

Planting and growth

The first choice a coffee farmer makes is what varietal of the coffee tree to plant. Two families of the coffee plant make up the majority of the beans available on the market: arabica (Coffea arabica), which makes up around 75% of the world's coffee crops; and robusta (Coffea canephora), which accounts for around 20% of them. Arabica coffees generally have a more complex flavor, and pretty much any single-origin coffee you encounter will be arabica. Robusta, on the other hand, is a hardier plant. It's more resistant to disease and variations in climate or elevation, making it a popular component in commercial blends. In a specialty coffee shop, you may see robusta utilized as one ingredient in an espresso blend.

Within the arabica family, there are dozens of what are called cultivars, or cultivated varieties, which you can think of as being similar to the varietals of wine grapes. The same cultivar could still taste drastically different depending on the growing conditions, but which cultivar the beans are grown from determines what range of flavors is possible.

The elevation at which the coffee tree is grown is arguably the most important factor in the developing the taste of the bean. Arabica coffees can grow at a wide range of elevations, from around 1,800 feet to around 6,300 feet above sea level; generally speaking, the higher-grown the coffee, the better the quality. Robusta can grow at a lower elevation, around 600 to 2,400 feet above sea level. The climate tends to be cooler in higher elevations; combined with the lower oxygen levels in the air, this makes the coffee trees grow more slowly at higher elevations, resulting in a smaller, denser bean (sometimes called "hard beans").

A coffee grown at a higher altitude is likely to be more acidic and aromatic, with more complexity in the cup. Coffee grown at lower elevations will be flatter overall, with less acidity and fewer flavor notes, making them good as a background presence in a blend. The fact that these beans grow more slowly also means that the yield per plant tends to be lower, which perhaps even more than the improved flavor tends to make them more expensive.

As a general rule of thumb, coffees grown at certain elevations will have certain specific flavor notes. Those grown at a very low elevation (2,500 feet above sea level or lower) tend to have a somewhat bland taste that may have earthy notes. Those grown at a low elevation (2,500-3,000 feet) are a bit more complex but still have a subtle, mild flavor. Medium-grown coffees (3,000-4,000 feet) tend to taste sweet and have a relatively low acidity. High-grown coffees (4,000-5,000 feet) have a slightly higher acidity that may give them a sweet citrus taste, though they often also have sweet vanilla notes or deep nutty tones, resulting in an often complex final cup. The most prized coffees, those grown at very high elevations (5,000 feet and higher) tend to have the highest acidity and can give you notes ranging from fruity to floral to spicy or wine-like, depending on what's done to the bean after it's picked.

While low-grown coffee is often seen as lower-quality, there are always exceptions to every rule. Coffee from the Kona district of Hawaii, for example, can't be grown at elevations over 2,000 feet; the island is far enough north of the equator that the climate is too cold at higher altitudes. Kona coffee is prized for its soft sweetness and low acidity, but the low density of the beans means it has to be handled carefully and can easily be ruined through over-roasting.

While the climate often goes hand in hand with the elevation, it also has its own influences on the taste of the bean. Especially important is whether the coffee is grown in shade or direct sunlight. In warmer regions, coffee plants can burn if exposed to too much direct sunlight, giving the beans a bitter aftertaste and flatter overall profile. Shade-grown coffee develops more slowly, giving it more complexity. The climate also affects the length of the growing season and at what point in the year the fruit is at its ideal ripeness. Even minor changes in temperature and rainfall levels can have a big impact on the quality of the beans.

The contents and quality of the soil also affect the bean. Not only will the correct ratio of minerals and nutrients encourage healthy growth of the plant but the minerals absorbed through the root will affect which oils and compounds are most prominent in the fruit and seeds. The same cultivar grown at the same elevation would taste very different if grown in an acidic soil, like one based on volcanic rock, than it would if grown in a more basic soil of limestone or clay.

These natural variations in climate, altitude and soil contents are also affected by the techniques the farmer uses to grow his plants. Farms in Central and South America are likely to prune their trees more regularly and use systems of irrigation and fertilization to encourage growth. Indonesian farms don't tend to prune their trees as regularly, and in certain regions of Africa, coffee beans are still harvested from wild-grown trees that undergo no cultivation at all. The more cultivation is employed, the more consistent the beans from that farm will generally be.

How much of this information you have about a particular bean will likely depend on where you shop. A coffee shop that roasts in-house is likely to at least be able to at least tell you which farm the beans came from, including its elevation and typical climate, as well as the bean's cultivar. As you get more familiar with different popular regions, you'll likely start to see patterns and trends in the taste profiles of beans from these areas.

Harvesting and processing

When coffee beans are harvested, the entire cherry is plucked from the tree. A variety of methods are then used to extract the seed from the fruit; the seed is then dried and sent away for roasting. Even on the same tree, the cherries will reach peak ripeness at different points throughout the growing season. Larger commercial farms often use mechanical harvesters, which can't tell the difference between a ripe and an unripe cherry. Since the oils in these seeds haven't been fully developed, coffee brewed from them will taste thin and weak; if they're not sorted out before processing they'll impact the overall quality of the final cup.

Even beyond picking out the unripe beans, how the coffee is sorted has an impact on the quality of the final cup. Both the coffee cherries and the beans inside them can vary in size, even if they grow on the same bush. This can lead to inconsistencies in the roasting if they're not separated by size. This can be done either mechanically or by hand; hand-sorting is more thorough, but machine sorting is more cost-efficient. One thing sorters look for are peaberry beans. This is a mutation found in a variety of different cultivars, in which the two halves of the coffee bean fuse together into one round seed. Peaberries are both smaller and denser than normal beans, which can lead to them getting charred if they're left in with beans of other sizes. When they're sorted out, however, peaberries are often considered to be of a higher quality than normal beans of the same cultivar, with a higher density that leads to better-developed flavors.

There are three main methods for processing coffee beans: dry or natural, wet-processed or washed, and pulp natural or semi-washed. The dry method is traditional and is in the modern industry used mostly by smaller farms. In this method, the whole cherries are spread out to dry in the sun for between 7 and 10 days. The cherry's skin and mucilage will become dry and brittle through this process, at which point they can be removed from the bean. Dry processed coffees tend to have a thicker body and a lower acidity. This processing method tends to bring out both rich fruity and earthy flavors.

A wet-processed or washed coffee is more common in areas that get high levels of annual rainfall. The picked cherries are put into vats full of water where they're left overnight to soften. These softened cherries are then run through pulping machines that remove most of the mucilage before being poured back into water vats and allowed to ferment. The beans are washed of any remaining traces of the fruit and dried either in the natural sunlight or in mechanical dryers. The taste of washed coffees is generally cleaner and brighter than that of natural coffees, with a lighter body and a sharper acidity.

The third processing style, semi-washed, is a hybrid between the dry and wet methods. The cherries are softened in vats like washed coffees but are then sent straight to the drying phase instead of going through the additional steps of pulping and fermentation. Some people find the semi-washed process gives the beans the best of both worlds, with a slightly cleaner profile than a natural coffee that has a bit more body than a fully washed.

Roasting

The inside of the coffee bean undergoes chemical changes during the roasting process that drastically affect its flavor. The sugars in the bean are caramelized; acids that were buried deep inside the bean are brought to the surface. How many of these changes the bean is allowed to undergo will determine the ultimate taste profile.

Beans that aren't roasted are called "green." If you tried to brew green coffee beans, you'd get a beverage that's sharp and vegetal, with bitter undertones like an over-brewed green tea. The roasting process is instrumental to bringing out the flavors we associate with coffee.

The lightest drinkable roast level is a cinnamon roast, named for the color of the beans at this level, not because the taste will have any traces of cinnamon. These roasts will have the highest acidity and a relatively weak body. The step above this is called a light roast or New England roast. It will be more aromatic and complex than the same bean at a cinnamon roast; the majority of beans need to be roasted at least to this level.

The next darkest is the medium or "American roast," so-named because of its popularity in North America. This is the level at which many beans are at their peak complexity, where the flavor oils have been fully extracted but the acids haven't burned off too much.

Finally, there are the dark roasts. The border between medium and dark roasts can be loosely drawn at the point where more than half the acids of the bean have burned off, replaced by a pungent, dark flavor and a fuller body. The lightest is called a full roast or Vienna roast and it is the level at which many beans are at their most aromatic. Next is the French roast, which is also called espresso roast because this is the level at which many beans are best-suited to that brewing method. The darkest roast is the Italian roast. It is the least acidic with the thickest body but with less complexity and aroma.

There are some beans that will taste good at a variety of roast levels, while others are more finicky and best-suited to a particular style. Beyond the accepted standards of the industry, roast level is in many ways a personal preference. Those who grew up drinking American-style coffee may find darker roast levels too pungent or bitter, while those accustomed to espresso would find a light roast thin and weak. Determining which roast level you prefer can help you choose your coffees as you're working on your ideal blend.

The Flavor Wheel

The Coffee Taster's Flavor Wheel was developed by the Specialty Coffee Association of America in 1995 to give coffee professionals a shared language for talking about the various tastes and textures of coffee, in the same way sommeliers talk about the taste and texture of wine. It has since become one of the most iconic resources for the coffee industry, helping both professionals and home enthusiasts to better identify the tastes in their brewed cup. If you're trying to fit the flavors of various beans together in a blend, the flavor wheel can help you to better identify the notes you're tasting, and which beans will complement each other the best.

The flavor wheel was updated in 2016, expanding the flavor options to be better-suited to the modern coffee market. If you're interested in seeing the wheel, you can look it up very easily on the internet, though you'll likely also find lots of variations as many coffee roasters will tweak the wheel to be better suited to their own roasts.

Not everyone's taste buds will be able to pick out the subtle notes in coffee without a little bit of work. Developing your palate is a skill, and like any skill it takes practice. You can do this not only by being mindful when you drink coffee, but also when you're eating other foods. Focusing on the taste of an apple or chocolate bar while you're eating it will help you to then identify those flavors in other things, whether that's a glass of wine or a cup of coffee. Don't only note how the object tastes; also pay attention to its texture and the way it feels in your mouth as you're eating it, internalizing the entire eating experience.

Coffee is a multi-sensory experience. You should pay as much attention to the smell of the coffee and the way it feels in your mouth as you do to the taste. When you're looking for the notes in the coffee, start by smelling the grounds. They'll be at their most aromatic immediately after they're ground, so if you can, it's best to grind the beans at home. You should also smell the brewed coffee as you're pouring it into your cup. At first, it may be hard to smell anything but just "coffee," but search for other aromas you recognize.

Some of the descriptors on the flavor wheel are pure tastes, and others are pure aromatics, but most of the items on the flavor wheel are produced through a mix of taste and smell sensations. Smell the steam of the coffee as you're taking a sip. Once it's cool enough, hold the coffee in your mouth and consider how it feels—if it seems to coat your mouth and linger after you swallow or if it's cleaner and more ephemeral. You could use terms like velvety, smooth, sharp, or dry to describe the feel. Words like pungent, tart and syrupy also describe some element of the feel, though they're also associated with a taste.

There is no one perfect cup of coffee. While there are some cultivars that most people consider to be superior to others, taste is ultimately a personal matter. As you taste your coffee with the flavor wheel, identify which notes you find the most appealing, and which you find particularly distasteful. Eventually, you'll be able to pick out which coffees you'll probably like, or which will go well together, simply by looking at the most prominent notes, rather than having to always find the right matches through trial and error.

Using the wheel

The flavor wheel is designed for you to be able to start from broad flavor categories and gradually pinpoint a more specific flavor. In the center ring, you'll see nine categories: floral, fruity, nutty, roasted, sour, spicy, sweet, vegetative, and other. Each of these categories is typically given a color association that can help you differentiate them, but these are not standardized and you can feel free to change them if another color seems more representative of the flavor to you.

Once you've located the basic category of the taste, move to the next ring, which gives you slightly more specific descriptors. From there, move to the third ring if you can. When you're first developing your palate, you might not be able to immediately pick out anything beyond the first ring. If you're having trouble, use the descriptors in the middle ring and work backward. For example, say you taste some fruitiness but can't tell if it's berry or melon. Imagine the taste of a blueberry and take another sip of the coffee, searching for that flavor. As your palate is further developed, you'll be able to skip this step.

You'll probably find it helpful to keep a tasting notebook while you're doing this so you don't forget what flavors you've tasted when you come back to the coffee to make a blend. You also don't have to limit yourself to the flavors included on the wheel. If you detect notes of mango or green tea, write those down. Each palate is different, and you want to note down what you taste, not what the coffee is supposed to taste like.

Floral flavors

Floral flavors tend to be fairly delicate and subtle, and in a coffee context, you're most likely to find them in lighter roasts. They're also more common in wet processed coffees, which have a cleaner, clearer flavor. Popular beans that tend to have fruity notes include Ethiopia Yirgacheffe and Guatemala Huehuetenango.

Florals are generally found more in the aroma of the coffee than the taste. Examples on the wheel include chamomile, rose, and jasmine. A black tea flavor is also considered to be floral since it often has a perfumey taste.

Fruity flavors

Fruity notes are some of the most commonly tasted in coffees from all around the world—which makes sense, considering the beans are the seeds of berries. Coffees that are dry-processed tend to be fruitier than washed or semi-washed coffees. You're also more likely to taste fruity notes in light roasts than in medium or dark roasts, and they also may be brought out more effectively by certain brewing methods; citrus notes are common in espresso, for example.

The fruity section of the flavor wheel is further broken down into the categories of berry, dried fruit, and citrus, with a catch-all "other" category for other flavors like coconut or apple; some flavor wheels also include the categories of stonefruit (such as plum or cherry) and melon. Light-roasted Ethiopians are known for their berry flavor, while Central American coffee—especially beans from Nicaragua—have a bright, clean citrus.

Nutty flavors

Included in this category are both nut flavors (like hazelnut, almond, or peanuts) and cocoa flavors. Both of these sub-categories are fairly common and are often more pronounced in medium and dark roasts. Milk chocolate flavors tend to have a smooth, velvety texture, while dark chocolate notes are often more bitter. If you're a particular fan of these kinds of notes in your coffee, check out beans from Mexico or Brazil.

Roasted flavors

As you might expect, roasted flavors are most common in dark roasts. Tastes are also included in this category if they have a toasted or smoky flavor. For some, flavors out of this category are too acrid or bitter; for others, a bit of a burnt taste is appealing, especially when complemented by a bright citrus or sweet caramel note. Subdivisions of this category include tobacco, malt, or grain tastes, as well as smoky or ashy notes.

Sour flavors

There are a couple different types of tastes included under the general umbrella of "sour." The first are the tart, pucker-inducing tastes that you probably initially think of. These tastes on the flavor wheel are noted as different kinds of acid, which is generally unhelpful for the casual taster. You may find it more helpful to associate this kind of sour with how it feels on your tongue—whether it's rough or dry or a bit sweet, like an orange.

You can also find fermented flavors under sour, which includes good tastes like wine and whiskey and undesirable tastes, which can indicate the coffee cherries were over-ripe or over-fermented. Sour tastes are fairly common in light-roasted and high-grown coffees from around the world, but well-fermented tastes are less common. Many coffees from Yemen have winey notes if that's a taste you're looking for.

Spice flavors

Spices like cinnamon and nutmeg make excellent complements to the taste of coffee, and you can sometimes also find these notes in the beans themselves. Some beans also have notes of clove, anise, or even black pepper, flavors that are often described as dark, warm, or pungent. These notes can be brought out through darker roasting but can be present in lighter roasts, as well. Beans from the Antigua region of Guatemala are often spicy, as are some Sulawesi beans.

Sweet flavors

As the coffee bean roasts, the sugars within it caramelize. This often gives medium and dark roasts a sweet taste, one that can either be light like honey or deep like brown sugar or molasses. Similar flavors like maple syrup or vanilla are also included in this category. If you're considering textures, you may find these coffees syrupy or viscous. When in a blend, they can provide depth for light fruity flavors, or balance out spicy and sour notes.

Vegetative flavors

This category can be a bit more difficult to describe to someone who's new to coffee tasting. Like sour, it is in part about the feel of the beverage, in addition to the taste. Also, like the sour category, it can include some flavors most people would consider unappealing. This includes a raw or under-ripe flavor, which can come from beans that are either picked too early or not roasted long enough.

If it helps, you could also think of this as the "green" category, where you find herbal flavors along with other vegetable flavors. Coffees that have a beany or pea-like taste would be called vegetal. Good "green" tastes are relatively rare in coffee, though you may detect them in some Indonesian coffees, especially those from Sumatra, as well as in some varieties from Kenya and Rwanda.

Other flavors

The catch-all category on the flavor wheel is where you'll find a lot of undesirable tastes. These include papery or cardboard flavors and tastes that are musty, dusty, moldy, or stale. The chemical sub-category includes bitter, salty, or medicinal notes. While some coffees have a pleasant woodiness or earthiness, like many Indonesian coffees, in general, the tastes in this category are considered to be roasting defects.

Regional Profiles

While some single-origin coffees are named for their cultivar—especially when that cultivar is particularly rare or prized—the majority will have more geographical labels, including the nation of origin and the specific farm or region where it was grown. All the factors discussed in the first chapter play a part in determining the specific characteristics of these different regions. While there will always be situational variations, beans from a given area will tend to grow at a similar elevation and with similar soil and climate conditions; farmers working in these regions will often employ similar techniques for growing, harvesting, and processing.

There are three primary coffee growing regions in the world: Africa, Southeast Asia, and Central and South America. These are obviously very broad areas, and you'll find a huge amount of variety within each region's production. All three areas produce very high-altitude coffee that's highly-touted by coffee professionals. Twenty years ago the vast majority of coffee that could be found in North America was produced in Central America or Colombia, but today Indonesian and African coffees are widely available in most regions of the United States and Canada.

The Americas

Over half of the world's coffee comes from the Americas. There are coffee farms in every nation of Central America, as well as Mexico and many islands of the Caribbean. In South America, Colombia, Brazil, and Peru are the major coffee producers. A lot of the cultivars grown in these regions are based on Bourbon, a cultivar that was developed in the Americas from the first coffee plant brought to the Americas from Ethiopia. It tends to produce beans that are mellow and sweet with a buttery mouth feel. Other cultivars derived from Bourbon include Caturra, Catuai, and Icatu; all three are found throughout Central America.

All the countries in the coffee-growing region of the Americas share a similar climate and grow their plants at a similar altitude. They also use similar processing techniques. Though the soil differs from region to region and the acid content of the beans can vary, you can usually describe American coffees as well-balanced and make a great base on which to build your blends. The highest-altitude American coffees come from Colombia and Guatemala.

Coffees grown in Mexico, El Salvador, Panama, and Nicaragua tend to do best a lighter roast levels. All have a relatively light body with a mild acidity. Mexican coffees, in particular, are known for their milk chocolate notes, while Nicaraguan and Salvadoran coffee tends to have more fruity and vanilla notes. Coffees from

Guatemala and Costa Rica have a bit more body and do well at a variety of roast levels. The Antigua region of Guatemala is known for having a spicy, almost smoky quality at darker roasts, while the beans from the Huehuetenango region are more delicate and floral.

Colombian coffee is similar to most Central American varieties. It's mellow and sweet, with a nutty finish, and has a moderate acidity. Coffee from Peru tends to be grown at very high altitudes and in a relatively acidic soil, making it bright and sourer than most coffees. It can be a useful ingredient in a blend if you want to add more high notes to the flavor profile. Look for the Maragogype cultivar for a slightly darker cup, or the Pacamara—a mix of Maragogype with Bourbon—for a brighter taste. You'll find the most national variation in coffees from different regions of Brazil, where there's a broader range of elevations and a wider variety of common farming practices. Naturally processed Brazilian beans are great in espresso blends because they have a tendency to linger in your mouth with creamy notes of chocolate.

Finally, there's the coffee of the Caribbean. Because they're island nations—and therefore relatively short on space—you won't find as many of these beans available on a regular basis, and the ones you do find are often expensive. Because of that, most people prefer to enjoy them as-is instead of mixing them into a blend.

Africa

Coffee originated in Africa. The plants grown today in the Americas and Asia are all derived from plants that originated in Ethiopia, which is one of the few places in the world you can find wild-growing coffee plants. The highest grown coffees out of Africa come from Ethiopia and Kenya, but you may also see beans grown in Burundi, Rwanda, Tanzania, Uganda, Yemen, and Zimbabwe. This is a large geographic area, meaning African coffees as a category don't have a general taste profile; instead, each country tends to have its own defining attributes, brought about by the nation's specific climate and typical processing methods.

There are a variety of processing methods used in Ethiopia, and while most of the coffee that's exported from this country is grown on farms, some crops are still harvested from wild-grown plants. The Heirloom cultivar is genetically closer to wild-grown plants than any other cultivated variety of coffee and grows predominantly in Ethiopia. Dry processed Ethiopians tend to have a syrupy body with lots of bright berry or sweet winey notes. Harar is a popular dry processed Ethiopian. Depending on the roast level, it can either have prominent blueberry notes or a deeper chocolate flavor that's great for espresso. Wet processed Ethiopians tend more toward a delicate, floral flavor, occasionally with notes of jasmine or black tea, with a lighter and drier feel on the palate. Yirgacheffe is the best-known wet-processed Ethiopia and has a balanced flavor, often with a bright citrus finish.

Where Ethiopian beans showcase the variety of African coffee, beans from Kenya tend to be much more consistent. Many of the farms in Kenya use the same cultivars, the most prized of which are the SL-28 and SL-34 varieties of the Kent cultivar popularized by British planters. Kenyans are typically wet processed and sun-grown. They often have an acidic savory-sweet flavor that's bold and juicy. There can often be a tomato-like flavor and acidity to Kenyan coffees, or else a puckering tartness similar to the taste of a cranberry or black currant.

Because Kenyans and Ethiopians are the most prominent African coffees, those from other nations are often compared to them. Tanzania, Rwanda, and Zimbabwe produce coffees that are very similar in overall taste profile to Kenyans but with a milder acidity. Coffee from Yemen tastes similar to a dry-processed Ethiopian but with a more fermented flavor that's incredibly complex, with notes of an aged brandy or wine. Coffees from Burundi and Uganda tend to have a lower acidity and heavier body and have natural notes of vanilla or chocolate that tend to come through most clearly with dark roasting.

Southeast Asia and Oceania

Like African coffee, that grown in Southeast Asia and Oceania exhibits a lot of variety from region to region. This is due to variations in both elevation and farming practices; there are a variety of different pruning, cultivation, and processing methods at work in the region. The highest-grown Asian coffees come from Papua New Guinea and the Sulawesi region.

Indonesian coffees are a lot more prominent than most casual coffee drinkers realize. The term "java" became synonymous with coffee because of the popularity of Indonesian blends in the early 20th century. Java is an island in Indonesia, and the coffee grown there tends to work well with medium and dark roast, with low acidity, a heavy, lingering body, and occasional woody notes. This is fairly typical of the Indonesian flavor profile. Many Indonesian coffees have a similar flavor to this, though they can also have a malty, stout-like flavor or a mushroom-like savoriness; the finish is often slightly bitter and lingering like unsweetened dark cocoa. The Sulawesi Toraja is typically processed with the semi-wet style, and has a darker taste than Java, with a spicy fruitiness.

Coffees from the Sumatra region are the main exception to the rule when we talk about the general taste of Indonesian coffees. They tend to be a very divisive coffee, with people either loving their unique taste and texture or hating it. Sumatrans can have a smoky, savory flavor or a fermented, sour fruitiness. The Mandheling varieties tend to be dry processed and have an earthy, dark molasses taste. Coffees of the Gayoland and Aceh varieties are more acidic, with a sweeter, plum or stonefruit taste.

Indonesia isn't the only Pacific nation to produce coffee. Vietnam is one of the few nations known for its robusta, and about 97% of the crops are of this less-heralded species. The coffees from Bali and Papua New Guinea have a similar profile; both tend toward the fruity and do best with lighter roast levels.

The Artful Blend

Commercial coffee roasters create blends for one of three reasons: for cost, for consistency, or for complexity. Blending less expensive coffees with pricier options lets the consumer experience those specific notes without having to spend as much to get it. Blends also serve as insurance against the yearly and seasonal variations of certain crops. If one coffee in the blend has a bad year, it can be replaced with something better without having too much impact on the final taste.

As a home enthusiast, the last category is likely to be more your purpose. Making blends at home is usually about combining different notes and taste profiles to create a more satisfying cup more than it is about trying to save a bit on your per-cup costs. This means you'll be shopping for your beans on the basis of their taste profiles, and how well you think they'll work together.

Even if you've studied up on different coffees and their typical notes, figuring out what goes well with what isn't always an easy task. One easy approach is to start off with a base coffee—one that you typically enjoy, or perhaps even your go-to choice. Think about what you would add to the coffee if you could. If it's a chocolatey dark roast, for example, you might want to add something with citrus notes to brighten it up, or maybe something with berry sweetness to mellow out the overall blend.

Find two or three coffees you think would bring these qualities into the blend. Brew up separate pots of all the coffees you plan to include in the blend then mix them together in varying ratios, keeping track of everything you add, until you've found the combination that tastes the most balanced. Using this ratio, whip up a batch of your blend and brew it, to make sure it still gives you the right flavor when you brew it. This method is preferable to blending the beans because it allows you to experiment and taste along the way, fine-tuning the blend without having to brew a new pot each time you make a change.

When you're first experimenting with blends, you'll probably want to limit yourself to two or three coffees maximum in each blend. Even when you are more familiar with flavors and pairings, you shouldn't try to combine more than five. The benefits of blending will start to be canceled out at that point, and you'll more often than not end up with a muddled cup.

You should consider how you typically brew your coffee when you're getting ready to make up a blend. Certain beans and roast levels are better-suited to certain brewing methods. Dark roasts tend to work well as espresso, but may be too bitter when brewed with a drip or pour-over method. Conversely, especially fruity, floral, or acidic light roasts that are bright and complex in the pour-over method can taste sour and thin from an espresso machine. The flavors of coffee tend to intensify as it cools, so if you're making a blend for a cold brew or iced coffee, a milder, medium roast is typically best.

While the popularity of Chemex, pour-over and Aeropress brewing at home has increased in the past few years, most casual coffee drinkers use some version of a drip machine. Drip machines are great brewing methods for mélange blends, a term that refers to combining beans at different roast levels. By using a mélange, you get the deep, roasted flavors of a dark roast balanced by the acid and brighter notes of a light roast, making for a more complex overall cup.

If you're still not sure where to get started, the recipes that follow can perhaps provide some inspiration. All are popular in some variation in the professional coffee community and can be tweaked as needed to suit your own tastes.

Mocha Java

One of the most classic flavor blends in the coffee world is the Mocha-Java blend, which is said to be one of the oldest blends still in use. You'll find that many coffee companies will have their own version of this blend. The exact contents and ratios will vary from place to place, but the overarching idea is the same:

50% Natural-processed Ethiopian, medium or dark roast

50% Sumatra or Java, medium to dark roast

The combination of the sweet, fruity flavor of the Ethiopian beans with the earthier, richer Indonesian coffee results in a cup that's full-bodied with deep chocolatey undertones. If you want to add more brightness and complexity to the flavor, you use two different Ethiopian varieties and a Sumatran or Javan. Start with a ratio of 1 part each then tweak until the flavor is exactly what you're looking for.

Italian Blend

The classic Italian roast is defined by its depth of flavor. It tends to be especially popular with North American drinkers accustomed to the darker roasts served by most large-scale restaurants and coffee shops. The trick with a good Italian blend is to capture those strong roasted flavors without losing the complexity of the overall cup or allowing it to take on a burnt or ashy flavor. A good starting recipe is:

70% Natural-processed Brazil, medium to dark roast

15% Robusta

15% El Salvador or Guatemala, light roast

Putting a bit of robusta into the blend gives it those deep carbon notes that you want in an Italian blend, while the use of a lighter-roasted and milder Central American coffee helps to provide some balance.

Drip Brew Melange

A mélange can be any combination of different roast levels, and if you want to keep things simple, coffees from the same country often complement each other. Using two roast levels of the same bean provides both complexity and balance, with the higher acidity of the lighter roast mellowed by the deeper flavors of the darker roast.

Melanges that integrate coffees from multiple nations can seem more overwhelming. You have to consider not only which regions' beans complement each other but which roast level is right for each component. If you're not sure where to start, try this recipe:

30% Colombian, medium to dark roast

30% Costa Rican, medium to dark roast

40% Kenyan, light roast

Both Colombian and Costa Rican coffees tend to have a caramel sweetness at darker roast levels that will provide a nice compliment to the bright acidity of the Kenyan without overwhelming its sometimes delicate fruity and floral notes.

Espresso Melange

A mélange can also be helpful when you're crafting an espresso blend. Pure light roasts can taste thin or sour, while pure dark roasts can taste ashy or muddled. A mixture of the two can give you the blend of bright citrus notes and deep, chocolatey finish that a good espresso provides. Try starting with a recipe like the following:

60% Mexican, dark roast

40% Natural Ethiopian, light roast

You can adjust the ratio up to 75%/25% if you prefer a darker flavor profile in your espresso. Using a natural Ethiopian has the added benefit of increasing the crema, but if an Ethiopian gives the final cup more fruitiness than you were looking for, try using a dry-processed Central American coffee instead.

Flavored Coffees

Some coffees have flavor notes that are more pronounced than others; some natural processed Kenyans and Ethiopians, for example, can have intense berry flavors, while some coffees from Mexico can taste powerfully of cocoa. Generally, though, the notes in coffee are more subtle. Most blends are designed more with an eye to the overall taste profile of the cup than they are to bringing out a specific flavor. If you want a coffee that actually tastes like vanilla or hazelnut, you'll need to add more than just different kinds of coffee beans into the mix.

You'll find a lot of different flavor options in the coffee aisle of the supermarket. Most of these commercial coffees get their extra flavor from a mixture of chemicals, which is adhered to the beans using a syrup or other binding agent. These residues can be left behind in your grinder and coffee maker, affecting the flavor of your other coffee for weeks afterward. What's more, manufacturers will often use their flavored coffee offerings as a way to get rid of their lower-quality beans, since the taste of this artificial flavoring is so strong it completely obscures all but the most powerful notes in the coffee. By adding your own flavorings, you can make sure you're only using natural ingredients and quality coffee beans. You also get to control the balance of the coffee to the added flavors, allowing the natural notes of the beans to shine through.

Coffee beans are naturally porous, absorbing flavors that are nearby. This can be a bad thing if you're storing your coffee beans in the freezer but is great when you're trying to flavor your beans, as they'll naturally pick up the flavors of anything you seal in with them.

There are a few different ingredients you can use to flavor your coffee, some of which can be utilized in a variety of ways for a different level and type of flavor. While none of these will linger in your grinder and coffee maker nearly as long as artificial flavorings, you may want to clean your equipment between flavors, especially if you're using extracts, nuts, or other ingredients that can leave oils behind.

If you use a burr grinder for your coffee beans, make sure to remove any extra spices, fruits, or nuts you've added to your beans, as they can damage or jam the burrs. You may even want to buy a small blade grinder to use with your flavored mixes. These can usually handle hard-shelled add-ins (and even if they are damaged, are much cheaper to replace) and they're easier to clean when it's time to switch to a new flavor.

Extracts

You'll find two kinds of extracts in the baking aisle: real and imitation. Real extracts are made by soaking mashed up ingredients like vanilla pods or cinnamon sticks in a liquid (usually some kind of alcohol) while imitation extracts are made by combining chemicals together that simulate the flavors. When you're using them to flavor coffee, you want to use real extract; imitation flavors are more likely to degrade over time and can have a bitter aftertaste.

Popular extract options that work well with coffee are vanilla, peppermint, cinnamon, coconut, orange, and maple. Use 3-4 tablespoons of extra for a pound of coffee. You'll probably find it easier to dump the beans into a large mixing bowl, tossing in the flavoring, and then pouring it back in the canister, rather than trying to add the extract right into the container.

Whole spices

Spices like cinnamon, cardamom, clove, and ginger pair well with the taste of coffee and can be used to add a bit of extra flavor to your beans. You'll get the most flavor if you crush the spices before putting them into the blend, especially with hard-shelled options like anise and nutmeg. Add about ¼ cup of crushed, whole spices for each pound of coffee beans and allow the flavors to mingle for 3-4 days before brewing.

Ground spices

Ground spices will have a very similar effect on the flavor to whole spices, but they'll need to be utilized a little differently. Rather than pour them in with the beans, you can mix ground spices in with your coffee after it is ground, just before you pour it into the brew basket. This can make it the perfect option for people who want to use a burr grinder but don't want to have to worry about picking the flavoring agents out of their beans. Add about 1/8 teaspoon of spice for every 2 tablespoons of coffee (about the amount you'll use for one serving).

The flavors listed in the "whole spices" section above are equally good options in their ground forms, but you also have other choices when you go this route. Pre-made mixes like pumpkin pie or apple pie spice complement the taste of coffee well, or you could use ground cocoa to enhance the coffee's chocolatey notes. Chicory is a root that's often ground up and added to coffee in France and French-settled regions like New Orleans. Originally used to stretch coffee supplies during lean times, it has a taste similar to coffee but adds a spiciness that pairs especially well with darker roasts.

Nuts

The oils in the nuts are going to impact the flavor of the coffee beans more than the aromatics. Because of this, you'll get the most extra flavor by crushing the nuts first to release those oils, and then tossing them in with the beans. Add about a tablespoon of crushed nuts for every cup of beans to start, and adjust from there to give you the intensity of flavor you're looking for.

Fruit

Fresh fruit has a lot of moisture, which can contribute to the growth of mold in your coffee beans if they're stored together. This leaves you two options if you want to add fruity flavor to your coffee: dried fruit or citrus rinds. Dried berries, cherries, or apricots can bring out the natural fruitiness of light-roasted coffee, though their flavor may be too subtle to be effective with fuller-bodied blends. Citrus peel, on the other hand, can be a great way to brighten up a darker roast. As with nuts, you should start with about a tablespoon for each cup of beans.

Go Blend!

The range of flavors that can be drawn from a coffee bean is truly staggering. It can give you everything from the bright acidity of citrus to the lingering bitterness of dark chocolate—sometimes in a single cup. Honing your palate and creating artful blends are both skills that you have to learn, and like any skill, they take practice to fully develop. Experiment with as many different kinds of coffee as you can and keep track of which ones you like and which you don't. Even as you hone in on which regions and roast levels tend to be most to your liking, go outside your comfort zone every once in a while; you just might find something that surprises you.

Most coffee shops that sell their beans in bulk will let you buy in any quantity. If you're getting a few different kinds to try out, a quarter pound should be enough to brew a few cups and get an overall sense of the coffee, and you won't run the risk of the beans going stale before you use them. Most coffees are at their peak flavor 7-10 days after roasting, so you don't want to let them sit around for too long.

Home-made coffee blends can also make great gifts, especially if you add flavoring. You can use extracts, spices, nuts, and fruits in combination to create your own recipes and make your blends truly unique. Remember that balance is the key. A more mellow coffee will be a better canvas for a lot of bold added flavors than one that already has a lot of depth and complexity.

Coffee is notoriously finicky, both as a plant and as a beverage. Slight changes in the growing conditions or roast times can have a big impact on the taste of the bean, and there will always be variations from batch to batch. Don't get frustrated if your blends don't turn out quite the way you expected, and be creative with your flavor combinations. With enough practice and experimentation, you can blend your way to the perfect cup.

Win a free

kindle
OASIS

Let us know what you thought of this book to enter the sweepstake at:

http://booksfor.review/blending

Want to

supercharge

your coffee knowledge?

Turn this page...

Also available by
Jessica Simms

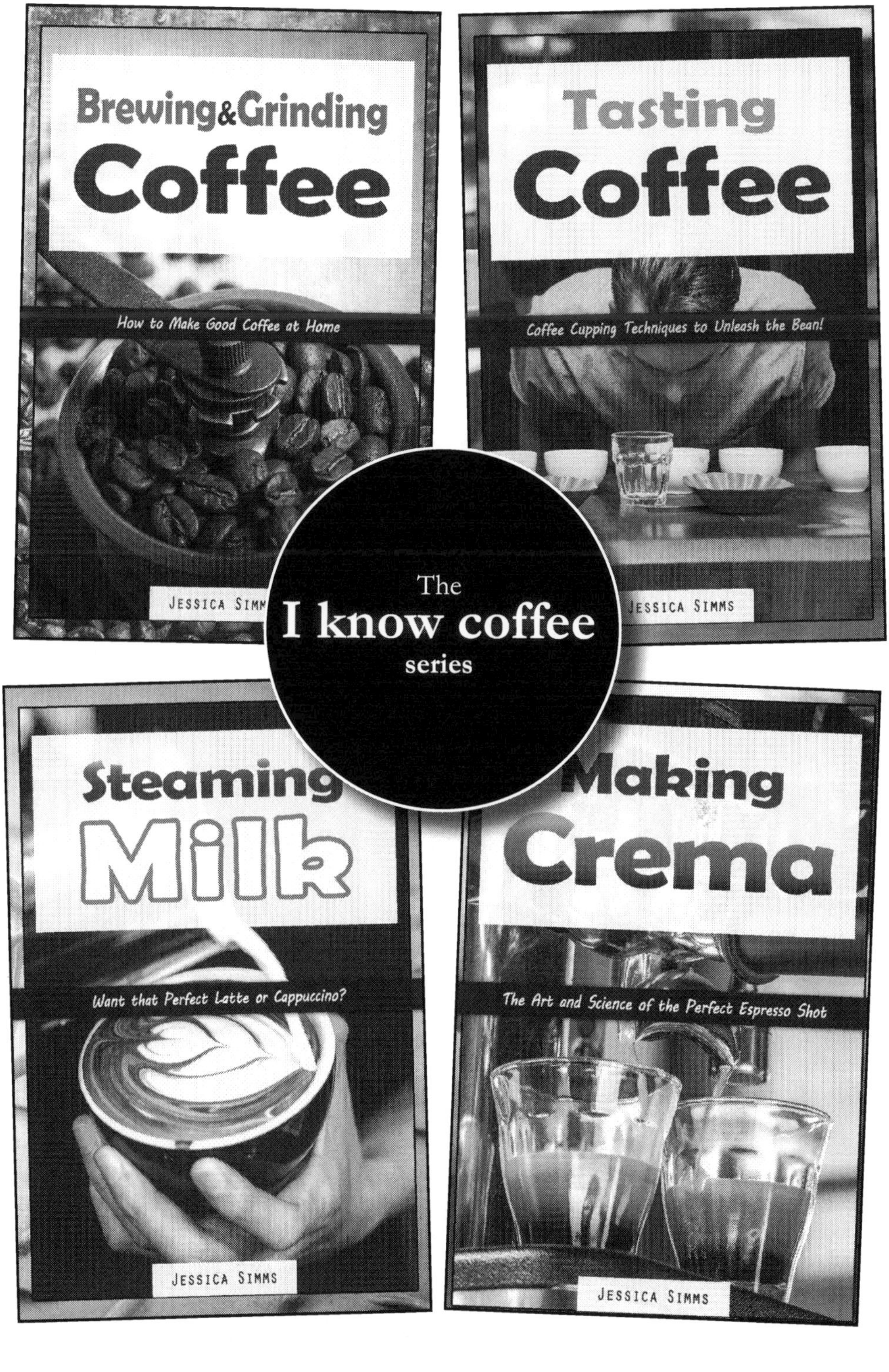
Brewing&Grinding
Coffee
How to Make Good Coffee at Home
Jessica Simms
Tasting
Coffee
Coffee Cupping Techniques to Unleash the Bean!
Jessica Simms
The
I know coffee
series
Steaming
Milk
Want that Perfect Latte or Cappuccino?
Jessica Simms
Making
Crema
The Art and Science of the Perfect Espresso Shot
Jessica Simms

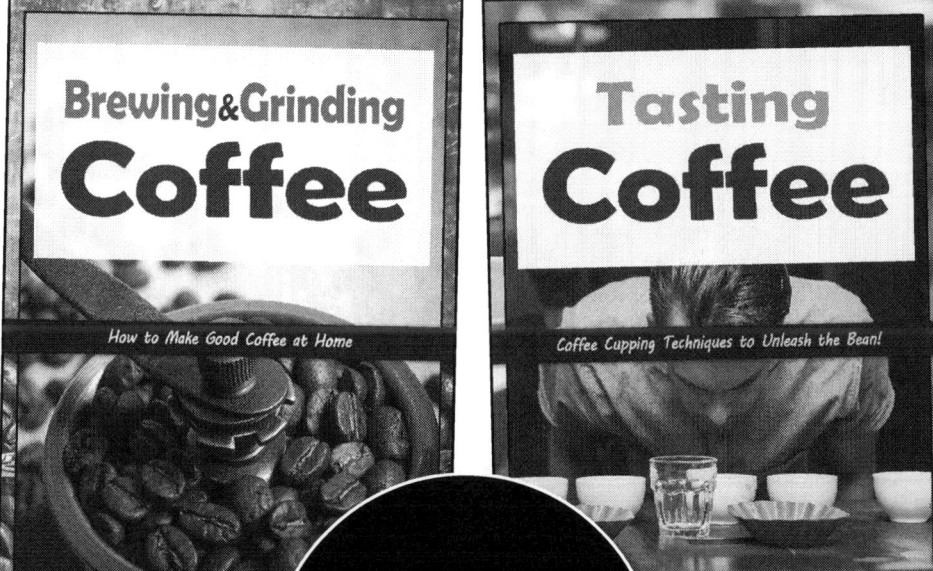